FRAYED LIGHT

WESLEYAN POETRY

Yonatan Berg

FRAYED
LIGHT

TRANSLATED BY JOANNA CHEN

Wesleyan University Press
Middletown, Connecticut

Wesleyan University Press

Middletown CT 06459

www.wesleyan.edu/wespress

© 2019 text by Yonatan Berg

© 2019 English translation by Joanna Chen

Manufactured in the United States of America

Designed and typeset in Merope by Eric M. Brooks

Library of Congress Cataloging-in-Publication Data
available upon request

Hardcover ISBN: 978-0-8195-7912-6

Paperback ISBN: 978-0-8195-7913-3

Ebook ISBN: 978-0-8195-7914-0

COVER ILLUSTRATION:
Anselm Kiefer, *Velimir Chlebnikov*, 2004 (detail)
30 paintings: oil, emulsion, acrylic, lead and mixed media on canvas
18 paintings: 75 x 130 inches (190.5 x 330 cm) each,
12 paintings: 75 x 110 inches (190.5 x 280 cm) each
Hall Collection, Courtesy of the Hall Art Foundation
Photo: Stephen White, © Anselm Kiefer

5 4 3 2 1

FOR
GEULA &
MAYA PAZ

CONTENTS

Part I

HANDS
THAT
ONCE
HELD
MANNA

LETTER TO THE READER

In conversations I cannot explain myself—still
an erupting mass of arrogant youth: fruits of conflict
with the body, an overflow of zeal trapped
inside, a decisive lack of seriousness,
traits acquired when I left
the grim corridor, too brightly lit with *mitzvoth*.
The constant urge to touch, I know,
means always to be thirsty.
I'm embarrassed by nudity, weeping, moments
of pure stupidity, gatherings with a family
that only asks to be left alone.
I try, time after time
to talk to the boy I could have been—
the engaged one, the generous, self-controlled one who pauses
before opening doors, allowing the dogs to run wild into the future.
They bark, my faithful friends of heresy,
of despair and self-denial, forever running inside me
with crude enthusiasm. Now, so it seems,
it's too late to change, too late
for caution. How I love the sound of glass
hitting the floor of the room, yes, you know it—
pushing through the midnight gate and beyond
to the flat surface, the silvery one,
the tired pipe organ of creation.
I apologize to each and every one of you

that I cannot touch, cannot reach out
to ease your pain, cannot hold you to me,
knowing I will ruin it all by saying something about the self—
something too flowery, too sophisticated. That being the case,
this letter becomes one blurry trail
of what, at day's end,
I really wanted to whisper in your ear.

UNITY

We travel the silk road of evening,
tobacco and desire flickering
between our hands. We are warm travelers,
our eyes unfurled, traveling in psalms,
in Rumi, in the sayings of the man from the Galilee.
We break bread under the pistachio tree,
under the Banyan tree, under the dark
of the Samaritan fig tree. Songs of offering rise up
in our throats, wandering along the wall of night. We travel
in the openness of warm eternity. Heavenly voices
announce a coupling as the quiet horse gallops
heavenward. We travel with the rest of the world,
with its atrocities, its piles of ruins, scars of barbed wire,
traveling with ardour in our loins, with the cry of birth.
We sit crossed-legged within the rocking
of flesh, the quiet of the Brahmin, the bells
of Mass, the tumult of Torah. We travel
through eagles of death, dilution of earth in rivers,
in eulogies, through marble, we travel through the silk
of evening, our hearts like bonfires in the dark.

PARTICULAR TIMING

Now my needy self, the wasted one, appears.
Now to be the one who crosses the dirt track
on his way to the ends of the evening, a boy
escaping home, close to silence.
Now to remember the young man entering
the Church of the Holy Sepulcher,
the smell of incense, the oil, flickering walls,
the great theological *ennui*,
the stones of the tomb blanching in damp darkness,
the great theological *ennui* and prayer,
now recalling prayer when pebbles of time multiply in pockets,
the stopping at night, the aching body,
the steaming chai, the silence of a chilly wilderness stretching
across an empty firmament, his name falling away from him.
Now when the body is located at the entrance to twilight,
when sleep is a churning ship in a conquering sea.
Now when the soul is a city, its courtyards ringing with young laughter,
the daily prayers of *shaharit, mincha, aravit* in the Beit Midrash, now
to recall Jerusalem, sweet hours before Shabbat, smell of Talmud,
of psalms, from whence I came and to where I am going
now, my own self picking the trampled flowers of mercy,
remembering the wandering gray of the monsoon, inaudible as love,
in crazed rain, in dance, in crazed rain hands opening in rain
crazed inside the laughter in rain singing in crazed rain

with dervish movements body swirling in crazed rain now
when the self is laid out, flung forward now
in light that gathers in a rented room by a bed in a night
of beaten copper, the faces. Now.

THE END OF NAÏVETÉ
(ISRAEL, 2017)

Things were different. We did not sit
in the presence of holy ones. Evening
sauntered along the street and
drunkenness reared up, startled,
from the tavern of our hearts.

The tree lost its mythical powers,
horses huddled at the edge of the earth.
The sniping light turned cold, winter came,
we continued, faces sealed. Only at night
did we sit down with our own names.

The yellow, the yellow above our heads.
The tone of air, the shape of time.
Some of us tried talking to one another.
Young guys hung around the square.
Oppression smiled sadly.

We laughed full-bellied, stretched out
on couches, holding on tight
to our increasing flesh. The rain began,
our words were not heard, we stayed
by the fire, lonely as love.

We told ourselves it would pass.
We put everything in place, near
the couches, the armchairs. On the balcony, flowers
spiraled toward the sun.

We told ourselves those were the bad days,
the high holy days. We cannot forever
await our destiny, we said.
Some of us stood in the square.
We sang songs in closed rooms.

We wrote letters, beautiful ones
with no address. We told each other,
your "I" is pure, blue
as happiness. We lay together, meaning
we bestowed love on each other.

We added nothing, nor did we take
away. There was no reason for them
to know we had already left.

MAP

My car turns at Hizme checkpoint, turns
into the village, passes pottery sellers,
the wall that punctures the narrative
of the hills, the barbed wire fence, olive trees
wrapped in the melancholy dance
of childhood. So why on earth cling
to this intimacy with the land, this fervour of ideology,
these urgent prayers and sense of sacrifice?
Why stay in the same cramped community
that prevents solitude and lust from washing over
the houses? And what about the births,
the constant preoccupation with scraped knees and bandages,
the warm milk before bedtime?
Further along the road is Adam, the first settlement,
and then the gas station,
my brother's vineyard,
the outpost of Migron—just
another day. There are cakes for every occasion,
concern for the sick or bereaved, synagogue
and gossip, bar mitzvahs and weddings.
So why on earth not? My car enters the settlement, turns
toward manicured gardens, the *mikveh*,
the school, the tiled roofs: the bourgeoisie
are the same wherever they live, busy
in their living rooms, tiptoeing over children and barrels of gasoline.

SETTLEMENT

The thorny bush of these hills
is utter sadness, a stubborn blast
that rises up in the face of youth.
Tin shacks paint the sun:
a bonfire of copper rags.

The evening descends with animal pain,
the *wadi* rolls it to the doors of our homes.
Children gaze over the fence at the hot throat of Ramallah,
the green pupils of their eyes journeying toward heaven,
signs of prayer that echo the moon.

Gathered into the night, we ask the fig
of distances, knowing that in purple there are secrets,
and that resin tortures the fingers.
Our ears fill with the sound of lead bullets bouncing
off blue doors, ricocheting across the *wadi*.

We ask to go there, to hear
their stories. We wake up for synagogue,
stained glass playing with the sun,
lighting birds on bare walls, creating shapes.

We wrap skin on skin, we cover our eyes
with one hand. We cannot understand
how our parents ignore the noise that ascends
the *wadi*, hot with the same memory,
olives dancing fruit into the ground.

RAMALLAH THROUGH THE WINDOW OF A BUS

Traveling through Ramallah, on our way to school—
early morning, the city preparing
for the day—stores just opening, steam
rising thinly from freshly made coffee.
Inside the bus our faces are glued to the windows,
our fingers coveting the fiery colors.
There is no fear, no recoiling—
the mechanisms of later life—
only curiosity, devoid of explanation,
toward more measured conduct,
toward the dusty, the gray. Teenagers walk
by the roadside, pushing carts piled high
with warm dough.
The grass grows wild, sprouting everywhere.
Nature's freedom of movement lies,
we know, in a different stance, less meticulous.
At night the clamor of weddings pierces the air,
singing of a faster pace, concealing
moments of interference,
a scanty no-man's-land of despair and longing.
Perhaps they are remembering the old house,
the lost garden. We do not fall asleep on the bus.
Our fingers drum of their own accord
to that other rhythm—loose and wild.
Years later, I would be lying if I said

there was no contempt back then, no
creeping fear, but it came from outside,
never from within, and it left us drumming
with confused fingers on steamy bus windows.

RETURNING

I am back to where slopes pour over
the Dead Sea, where the sun extinguishes
the prickly rose, leaving only olives to burn silver.

My father sits in the dark, a spoon of honey
in his mouth. My mother hugs herself,
thinks of her parents, far away.

The cherry trees are covered in pink snow;
my dog gazes with yearning at the deer.
All this trickles into the dark.

On the other side of the valley a bonfire burns,
a wild voice rises, a Middle Eastern one.
Someone is going to synagogue.

The *muezzin*, the moon and the barking. Trembling
overtakes the fig, sown with light through branches,
through approaching forgetfulness.

All this has passed. Only the fumes remain.
I sit on my childhood bed, my parents separated,
my dog dead, the synagogue locked.

But light sleeps over dips in the *wadi*,
and the child comes out of me,
sits under a tree,

clods of earth between his fingers,
and the same hot summer ripens the air,
moving nectar into my eyes.

FRIDAY MARKET

The air surrenders to December's lucidity,
the sloping road is heavy with fate.
We travel the day with a sense of urgency.

My pockets are full of scraps: remarks
on Milosz's captive spirit, notes on Hebrew poems,
a verse I ripped out from my rabbi's book

of loneliness. The market entrance is crowded
with missionaries, a two-bit folk singer,
strips of *tefilin* curled on a table, boys

in youth movement shirts, explanations
full of passion for abandonment.
The air within us surrenders

to Shabbat eve. Rain passes through,
drawing out hidden colors, the smell of fruit
hanging in the air, the peddler's cry.

I am a person with no homeland. I stop,
inhale the sobbing light as it lands
on the soft edges of my face.

DISTANCE

I walk through the settlement, years later,
Through the quiet of Shabbat afternoon, reading
slogans at an empty bus stop. *The blood of Israel is not in vain!*
No to destruction! Ahead of me rests a broken wooden bench,
The Edom Mountains and the Dead Sea, thorns and
Mediterranean light. A youth slips away to synagogue,
his lips forming words of prayer: "For though my father
and mother have forsaken me, God will take me up."
From the youth club, voices of ideology rise up.
I recall journeys to school through Ramallah,
a song on the radio about a boy whose eyes
are scared and hungry, a child my own age
sitting on a stool outside a mosque.
The trees in my father's orchard stand naked,
and I return home, hands stained with the blood of cherries.
I face the window, a bonfire burns, sounds from a wedding.
Is there a certain moment when the wandering begins?
Shabbat table, a white cloth, red wine, challah, but also fear
of my father, violence piercing through.

I walk past a lookout point with benches and a plaque for the dead,
but once this was a kingdom of rocks and insects
where a single ruler spent whole afternoons wandering the hills
until the shouting began and I ran home for dinner.

Someone comes out of a house on his way to evening prayer.
Do you remember returning from the yeshiva,
the path leading up to the house, the stairs, and all the times
you climbed them in uniform, the gun bouncing on your back,
the stench of oil, all the times you cursed out loud,
having nothing more appropriate to say, before death.

The sun begins to waver, the Edom Mountains fold pride
into fire, the Dead Sea extinguishes itself
but the worshippers multiply, returning from prayer.
After they threw me out of the yeshiva
we descended the mountain at dawn, talking theology,
thinking first love into the cool of the day.

For a minute I am here, dancing under the moon, singing
"Blessed is your Maker, your Creator, Blessed is your Possessor."
Years afterward I danced under the moon, naked and hallucinating,
Goa, Gokarna, Varanasi, Taganga, Itakra, Ika, Banyus:
a series of pledges in the distance.
On the way home, it turns cold.
A single car violates the Shabbat. Something drops, disappears.

Part II

DUST RISING FROM THE BLOW

THROUGH THE EYES OF RAMALLAH

To wake up, to see the copper packages and say
home. An ugly flow crawls along the land,
turning it to mud the way thought shapes the future.
Dogs blessed with wandering return from the hills,
congealed blood of deer on their lips:

This is how the present works. A defeated
kitchen table, silence between water
and faucet, fresh bereavement notices,
anger pacing the rooms. To me

the red-roofed houses of the neighboring hill
look like fists. Children memorize the book of fury.
Strips of no-man's-land between youth
and family give birth to deeds of no return.

This is the first lesson in the logos of humanity.
The second lesson is the moment of ashes:
the same veiled shock on the same gray faces,
the same creaking door,
the same tenderness.

THE MOTHERS

The melancholy mothers come to me in sleep,
demanding their sons.
I hold my head in my hands,
I turn my back on them.
The one with a Leviathan circling his eyes sits down
to write. The melancholy mothers dissipate
like milk, congealing into statues.
I have no energy to count the dead
as they pass, one by one.

The moon fades, leaving only dust.
Did someone see the horizon,
the luscious tree before the sin?

The melancholy mothers scratch the air,
their fingernails of bereavement breaking,
tearing their clothes,
flowing onto cold marble.

Their boys lie over the *wadi,*
crumbling soil between their fingers,
beyond the houses,
beyond the candles.

AFTER A NIGHT IN THE ALLEY OF WORSHIPPERS

The point is not the frayed light of six a.m.
or the barking of dogs, half-crazed by the scent
of blood, who we drove away.
Nor the fatigue from a night spent deep
in death, the network that only now falls
silent, the shouts from the platoon above, identifying
bodies, the reflex that all this was to be expected.
The point is not how they lay there, after
the dogs lunged into them, their faces
distorted, their wounds festering, strewn together,
black-garbed, the dirt of the road stained darker
by their blood. One held the glimmer of a smile,
not wicked or revengeful, just lost.
The point is, I volunteered, and Vish, the officer,
was my friend. But when we got there I could not,
I simply could not. To this day I see Vish and a soldier,
shoving them into the armoured truck. They are dropped,
are dragged, I don't have a better image for all this:
the bodies dragged, dropped,
over and over.

OCCUPATION OF THE LAND

The transition is noiseless, devoid of enthusiasm,
all gentleness extinguished as strength loads the face
with tension and expectation. Land and home, land
and home they recite, accustomed to cold steel
in delicate hands that once held manna. Forty years

shudder momentarily, hastily dissipating,
air crushed by voices of response —
the motion of a body about to meet a body
always begins in passion.
Crowded, cramped together, trying to transmit

warmth but failing, finding themselves
alone. I see the first onslaught, shouting to banish
terror, raising an arm to feel
the heaviness of steel, abandoned,
sensing how a new coldness — fury — pressures the lips,

the eyes, getting used to the body anew.
Their faces are fixed on Joshua —
he too is shouting, eyes closed,
walking into the land,
leading us through the eternal hoop of fire.

THE FIGHTER SPEAKS

A vast silence envelops me.
My voice empties slowly, my hands are tired.
In whose name do we move forward, passing through cities?
We warm each other up, shouting,
houses falling around us,
alleyways burying us.
All the while the eye is open, and the hand is on the trigger-
bar. I want to sit down,
do nothing with my body,
let it melt in the blast.
Will someone atone for me, lift up
my head and whisper to me?
Quietude passes through me as we attack.
I want to sit down, take in the light breeze,
the scent of trampled herbs,
to isolate myself in my own body,
held by a summer that opens the earth with warmth.

JENIN

Houses crumpled into each other, dirt roads
and jostling antennae: a sealed, airless mass.
From the balcony of the captured house we see the hills
of the Promised Land, dotted with prickly roses.
The family living here has fled but
they always leave something small behind—
traces of dinner, a dripping faucet—
now we are surrounded by dryness.
Later, between alleyways,
I warm myself thinking about my own home:
tiled roofs, a woman leaving her house,
still wet, releasing the perfume of virginity
into the air. I return to the sound of a stone
rolling down, the *muezzin*,
someone cursing quietly in the dark.
After midnight there is only fear,
a ceramic flak jacket, a desire to sleep, to see the woman
singing to herself, sitting on a white chair in the garden
and then, the boy who went out, advancing in silence along the road
and his eyes, black and moist, looking at me fearlessly as he steps along—
filled with hatred, filled
with loathing, and then I glance away,
sensing the pack of dogs
within me, far from home,
violence directed by the barrel of a gun.

REMEMBRANCE

Despair wraps itself around your name.
For a moment I am alarmed, cannot reconstruct
the intense jawline that held the face.
Time is like ash,
like the constant flow of rivers,
like ridicule.

Winter darkens the house,
dancing on wooden drawers.
How can we be rescued from forgetfulness,
from daily habits, from long mornings
in which we dress ourselves
in respectable appearances as if there is no
deserted, dirty hallway below.

How can I bring you to the balcony,
to the spring festivities,
to wine and walnuts, a book of poetry,
to the spectre of a street busy with itself.
How can I mourn the distance of years,
of waste, of your silence
seeping into the earth?

POSITIVE IDENTIFICATION

I stand here, God's tumult behind me.
You lie on a stained gurney,
covered with a tallit, your face exposed,
praying with slumped organs.

I whisper breaths. *Come breaths,*
I say, but they do not come,
only nights where you appear illuminated,
fashioned from earth and weeping parents.

I nod my head as your name is uttered.
Are you sure?
Night collapses in the chest, a jackal appears
above the Judean Hills, salty

from one end to another, dry-skinned,
dry-mouthed. The sound of a harp filters
the air, and its strings make way
for your face, ruddier than ever.

HEBRON

I return from the funeral, my uniform
stained with dust, my throat ashen.
First the military rabbinate,
a cold corridor, then the drive
to Jerusalem, coffin between my legs.

Everything is burnt by the roadside.
We do not look at each other,
not even when the coffin is hoisted
onto our shoulders, heavy
with youth and laughter.

The stickiness of family, hand
in hand, *kaddish*,
fists, hard earth,
Hebron inside us.

POST-TRAUMA

It was that night, 2006. We went down there
shouting, opening bottles with our teeth,
mixing drinks. Raz wandered off to get dope,
whatever he could find. The pupils of our eyes were huge
from hunger, too. We dropped into a bar and then another one,
raucous and laughing. No one meant it, afterward,

in the bathroom. We licked the edge of a credit card, left cigarettes
burning. The street of Allenby, then Herzl. I arrived at your place,
a room shaded like a sketch. Necklaces and bracelets hung off a peg
on the wall, miracle of shapes and colors. You did not ask
why, you brought water. You sat next to me. We had sex,
not with any great fervor, not with humor, but with the instinct

of survivors, hoping that something
might come of it, in the body, in the closed room.
Your shoulders, the silence, the weak light of the lamp, I left
without saying a word, to the sea at Jaffa. I drank a beer
and then another one, and facing the rising sun as it struck
the sand, I realized what happened in Hebron.

AFTER THE WAR

The last ships have been defeated, the sea resumes
talking to itself. A black century
sinks behind the hills,

a convoy of broken iron vehicles
waits at the entrance to the city, rust consumes
the golden hyssop.

Evening is translated
through a curtain, a window box.
We do not know how to undress slowly

but at night we wear perfume.
The land returns from betrayal, casting
events into the horizon. A shivering

wind reveals the dance of the fields.
Black shoes, leather gloves—
everything is left to decompose.

We buy white cloth.

Part III

AN
ISAAC
MOMENT

IMPROVISATION

Moscow, 1977. The roads are empty,
frightened by every stare, every parked car,
the trace of a shadow behind a stone wall and my father
moving along swiftly, like a hint.
He carries a sheet of paper, or perhaps knows
the address: an improvised synagogue,
whisperings, a cup of something or maybe
just that same sense of stuffiness, the ancient self
meeting the contemporary one.
Everything is done in haste, except the tune,
or maybe it's just the rabbi, the only one
who knows the notes and the words, who closes
his eyes, sensing how the dust, each musical beat,
is removed, as if by a soft cloth,
and something muted yet dense
is revealed in the way they turn to face the world.
They get up, they each return
to their exercises in evasion, their crowded apartments
where they only curse in secret.
I see my father, swallowed up in an alleyway.
Was he honest enough to hear
his own sad coyote
still wandering restlessly along dirt roads
like a panicked, hungry breath,
through the changing of seasons, and countries?

His voice rumbles above the earth,
seeping into the dust, the dust that surrounds
the heart of God, and to which is added
the broken sigh of a Jew.

ODESSA

These silent streets,
these heavy houses, electrical wires
doubled over in the wind,
the gloomy sea, waiting quietly
to pounce,
the crowded buses,
sprawling markets, overladen,
the raised orchestra stand
in the middle of the park,
the long mall marked
by countless footsteps,
the Opera House pulling toward it
all the streets, commanding respect
for the city, and yearning,
the universities planted with a wisdom
that recognizes the need for young voices
packed with passion, packed with
student rebellion, the long promenade packed
with drunks and teenagers, the Potemkin Stairs,
the power of film to turn stone
into symbol,
the port that releases outstretched arms
languidly embracing shipping containers,
the statues of Pushkin, of Babel,
the tram with its rusty metal wheels

buzzing with electricity,
the hotels, their couches and beds, a balcony
and closed roofs between buildings,
over cars,
cafes and bars, restaurants
and clothes stores
all of them
brimming over with the ghosts of Jews.

A LATE LANDSCAPE

When gray buildings appeared in the window,
decorated with white down, we talked.
Chimneys drew snakes of smoke, your hand
lay open there, as if asking for touch. The river
twisted with the lethargy of water and women strode

beside it toward a gloomy horizon, heads covered.
There are no young men in the city,
only the sound of departing trucks.
Again you asked my other name, written on the wall
of souls, the one used on days of hunger. At home

in Maale Adumim, it is almost dark.
The dog flops on the carpet, a plate
of apple slices remains untouched,
cups of tea have grown cold.
There is no connection to the northern city through the window.

In the Judean silence, what lies ahead of you has changed shape,
orphanhood is an outlook, a decision of the curve
of your back against a drooping evening, a colder one,
an hour when the trickery of life is close to complete clarity,
when the staircase is visible

in full light. This is why we now sit,
and in the window this scene arises:
a boy skims stones on freezing water,
places a hand to his cheek, as you do now, when we fall silent,
trying to hide the twist in the path.

VISITATION

My father does not sleep at night,
his face is an ancient ship,
relaxing its sails as the home port appears.

His silence is full of the streets of the city
he left behind, where women decorate chairs,
where nakedness soothes,
wiping clots of factory from the brow.

My father looks at Jaffa, fingers the snow of Odessa.
The voice of the *muezzin* calls the worshippers to prayer
and I lean over the edge of the rocks,
whispering a request for the days remaining to him,
to live with a sense of home,
to take long walks through memories.

"Time to go," my father turns to me:
The moment of separation approaches.
On the port steps, the light of night descends.

FATHER

My father walks with difficulty,
his body demands he lay down the bundle
but his thoughts continue to run ahead.
He endured the big freeze
of the previous century, and in early afternoon,
stained with beer, I see how the factory
continues to dance smoke out of his mouth.
We talk about everything under the sun, everything
but family. Now he puts down the bundle,
begins polishing the broken menorah.
He is tired, the writing of summaries
begins, I add one of my own:
you survived it with the only heroism possible —
a clean shirt no matter what,
bread for the children, never take revenge,
never ask for charity, never give up
even if this is the twentieth century —
the summing up of stupidity and fear.

PSALMS

On Sabbath afternoon the air was quiet.
We strolled toward the Sephardi synagogue, the hills
were filled with afternoon and beyond, the Dead Sea
shimmered, burning with salt, thick with death.
Rabbi Avi Sasson stood before us,
his voice filling the curves of the stone
with psalms. We sat down. Summer switched off
and we gave ourselves to the same cave
where praises cover the decay
of our lives—our parents arguing, journeys through Ramallah,
the idea that around us hung
a permanent, burning growl of injustice:
the shifting of Israel and Palestine's tectonic plates.
So we begin to chant with him,
moving our bodies in imitation of the adults,
closing our eyes for a moment,
discovering a cave in a cave—
the unfamiliar flow, permanent inside us,
of a weak, white light, like an unknown
morning, devoid of name,
in which we stand, pointing
beyond the white-bearded image
of God. But all this vanished
when the rabbi handed us our reward—
the candy wrapper was crushed hastily,

chocolate melted into Sabbath,
Sabbath merged into toffee,
a sticky hand, a mouth, a white shirt.
My entire childhood collected into five minutes
outside the Sephardi synagogue,
hungry and surging with sugar,
faithful to the white beard, to the soft voice, faithful
until this moment to the sugared silence of the Sabbath.

TO MY MOTHER

You ask with your eyes
where autumn and savagery come from.

You hand me a clean handkerchief,
ripe figs. I have been moving away

for years, finding you before bedtime
tucking the blanket around me, singing

of angels who watch over children.
How can I explain to you the animal

that growls within, the same rose
pinned to every hour, staining the light

red, sinning in thought, me
sitting by the tree, sketching

its movements, the olive releasing
stars one by one, the movement

of your hand, signaling me
from afar, to come back.

Part IV

WATER
PIERCES
ITSELF

ADAM AND EVE

A full season, compressed.
Nectar blooming
through naked hours,
kissed without remission
by an evening that is all quiet blessing:
water pierces itself in order to gleam.

What pursues this day that comes and goes?
What shakes and howls with hunger,
utterly trapped

in continuous plots
of fertility,
intervention in the air,
bursting forth with the despondency of fruit trees?

Why do hands seek
to sever themselves from touch?
A slithering, weeds trampled en route to us,
the night snake slips away whispering
abandonment, whispering poison.

CAIN

I see you now, years later,
crushing air into your body, leaning toward me
in a gesture of consolation, the field quivering
around us, abandoning itself
to insects and sun. I walk off, watching you
begging to return to the crumbling soil,
watching you wet it with glittering hands,
hearing it answer, rising up toward you.
An unfamiliar feeling emerges,
the look on your face, taken aback
but still believing, your hands
still moist, still smooth,
unresisting as blood spurts and violence revives.
I hold you again, my own face already pointing upward, looking
for a God who can see us, one who can intervene.
But no voice is heard as you collapse onto the soil,
as you touch it, trying to remember, grasping for an explanation.
I stand, rooted to the spot, even when you stop moving, then retreat—
compelled to find a place where the soil is dry,
emptied of water—a place as parched
as the dryness within me.

ABEL

I saw you approaching, the day clear.
You walked with heavy steps, ready
for the journey. I saw no violence inside, nothing
but vulnerability, looking around
for a place in which to reinvent yourself.
We sat down, you remember that, reducing
ourselves, believing this was how to get close. We spoke
the way we do when there's a storm brewing inside—
about the weather, the goats, the coming harvest—
each one tiptoeing around the other. Then your muscles seized up
and I saw how it rose up inside you, glistening and dynamic.
Hatred made you beautiful.
We parted company, you yearned for more
than I could give, yearned for a father who could promise
all this would pass. You held me tight,
wrenching the generosity out of us, the blood,
the eyes, the breath. I fell, watched you receding
into the distance, and only then did generosity pass through me,
barely perceptible, searching for your face,
gleaming, but you disappeared, or perhaps I did,
drowning in white.

NOAH

The land washes over with grief,
a strange blossoming
as they lope toward each other,
conceding to openness.
My own body slackens, adopting the milk
of dawn hours, the small altar:
a heart blackened by incense and prayer.
Every evening I speak to the void,
seeking to decipher
the voice that passes through us:
a riddle we fail to understand.
We will not be swayed.

The deluge is a frightened breath,
the feverish touch of life itself.
I stare at them until I see the cries
concealed in their throats.
Yes, I cheated.
Their breaths burn like summer
and I am left to walk
alone, engraving their names
on the ruined altar.

ABRAHAM

His quiet life was undermined.
Music surely broke out from somewhere, the way it always reports
for duty when we are abandoned. The Midrash was wrong—
it was not the partial strength of the sun and moon that released him,
we do not look for power or presence,
on the contrary—empty pockets, the conduit of days waning
in the watery depths, invisible, devoid of loyalty—
only here does faith emerge. We relinquished rags of language
with ease, surrendering to the unknown, finally ready
to embrace the chasm. He meandered along, pushing further
and further toward the empty, conversing swiftly
with that same music, asking it to come back.
I see his face contorting with each blow,
dancing between the statues, falling to his feet,
raising dust. We enter into a dance like this, each of us
knowing suddenly the lie that is home, each of us
hearing the distance that awakens with alacrity within,
How the music rouses itself, preparing its tools, opening the night,
placing fire in our hands. The room, the kitchen, the settlement,
I let them raise smoke as I walk off, thinking of Abraham,
muttering like him, dancing like him while the dust dissipates,
leaving for a land made of music.

SARAH EXPELS HAGAR

An empty tent, heat and bitter laughter. The body
is unwilling to open, life happens far away.

Dreary months snuff each other out.
He returns to me, flaccid, drenched in the fragrance

of pleasure and abandonment. She moves there, in all places,
calling to him with mellowed scent, pinching the air

with balmy bells of passion. Beauty takes its leave of me,
relinquished over the years, in that internal jump-off. Canaan

burns in the distance, I grant them each other
and now nothing remains to grant me

presence. I conceive within this,
nourishing the fury, the jealousy. I curse her, ready

for battle, ready to refuse what has grown inside me until this day.
Suddenly strong, I stride toward her,

my hand fisted, laughter erased, disappearing behind the last tent while
I take hold of him, lean into him

as his eyes follow her. She is already thirsty,
containing her sons, who wait in the trenches for mine.

INVERTED SACRIFICE (ISAAC)

Each of us has an Isaac moment:
The father, trapped in a tired body,
continues forward, while the son unties
the rope of family, striding forward,
teaching himself (Abraham
remains slaughtered, Isaac sheds the skin
of love). Separation—the real hero of sacrifice.

RIVKA

|

Deserted herds.
An empty bowl of stew.
With one stroke night falls
and I hear the hunter's voice.

|

My hands bless air.
Dense wildness in folds of cloth,
long periods of expectation
lowered in my eyes.
My galloping sons.

|

Lost infertility, why did I listen
to the supplication of flesh?

Now red hours
educate me.

|

By the water wells
a naked hand
in love with thirst.

A girl exits me, so
fresh,

by morning she stops
and extinguishes her name.

RACHEL

Walking along the morning,
fingering the seven years,
still waiting, still waxen.
Once I spoke to you naïvely, believing
in justice, training my body to open out.
I am ready to wait,
but the lie disappoints me: your need to move among us
uncommitted, amazed anew
at the intensity of our feelings, refusing to look.
Yes, we are quick to anger,
waving our little hands around
in fury and desperation, waiting for you,
a face that is fleeting,
bursting forth too quickly for any repair
of empty hours.
I know my sister was needier than I,
and her body craved this gravity.
I only ask why you did not speak—I
would have given you devotion.
How can we talk to you when you sit
with your back to us, legs together, incompetent,
restless, friendless
in the void.

YOCHEVED

His voice still rests on my face
but my song continues to sink down.

Why was I not permitted to wear the evening hours,
to whisper to him as he fell away,

to live within the confused flickering of his eyes
before he knew the body's sorrow.

Do not tempt me with the gift of eternity.
So many mothers lean like me

against the abyss, emptied out,
drying the colors of the day

on long benches, faithful to expectation.
I am expelled, distancing each hour

from his body, his bare legs surely growing cold
as his mouth continues wandering through the air.

His name blossoms now among the many slaves,
his hands rise up to announce the morning to them

while I hear nothing,
his image wiped from my memory:

only the brightness remains,
the light his face engraved upon my name.

JOB

It's always leaking and cold,
out of place, against you.
They organized it, the collusion was clear:
Death, arrogance, violence. You insist,
you grip the banister, drag yourself along,
friendless save for that bitter one who talks
incessantly, even when you are alone.
Hours are snatched from us, trampled upon,
outside the city an army camps, the rocks in place, the drum calls.
Job was right, there is no righteousness.
A pious person and an evil one — human formulas,
a fumbling in the dark, a pause while everything
turns, gambling one season for another, light for dark.
But Job beckons me too,
beckons us all with the same stubbornness. We did nothing
wrong. Faithful in spite of everything, silent when evil
raises flags in the avenue,
waiting worriedly for our brothers to return.
It is not because of us that winter lengthens, not because of us
that flowers are lain on cold stone.
None of this was created in our name, we asked for
nothing but morning, the clean voice of children,
the muttering of God's name.

THE PROPHET DEVORAH

Day breaks under the tree, and cold rises
from the ground, meeting their twisted faces.
I answer them, asking them to stop
but they gyrate toward each other, angry, expelled from the Garden,
ensuring no one will have it easy.
I set out for war, urged them
to join me, promised victory. I see everything:
those who remain lying down, slowly uniting with the earth,
crushing empty soil between their fingers, those who stay at home,
looking out at the vineyards,
trampling clusters of grapes, drinking the wine, stained
by betrayal. I see God,
the one I glorified, already tired, looking
at the land going up in flames, confused, as if
he had not imagined such a thing, the swiftness with which they charge,
as if calling him, asking him to look.
I see mothers waiting by the window,
they will not return, the scent of milk no longer
envelops them like a shawl.
I see violence, the way it arouses us, bestowing
power, bestowing ascension and then disappearing,
satiated, leaving us heavy, circumventing
ourselves, unable to enter.

JUDAH THE MACCABEE

We're restless, like any other tribe.
Kingdoms rise and fall. This is why we're in love with the sea,
the mountains, our gaze turned even further away, believing
in the fluttering within, the need
for perfection. The hours are lusterless,
quickly covered in dust.
They drew closer to Jerusalem—the
highest mountain of all.
They kissed the golden vessels,
felt close to what lies beyond,
lit candles, observed how flames
paint mystic ceremonies on gold.
They sang, knowing that only in singing are we full citizens
of that other continent.
They roused themselves for battle, until Elasa.
No, there is no land beyond the land
no milk and honey flowing down the hillside, staining the earth.
There is only desire
to mark eternity,
to beat time,
even through fire.

JESUS

We need the Galilee to fathom him: a stubborn movement
upward of the land. He leans forward, reaches out,
offers bread: before fury, the hand does not know the fist.
We need Jerusalem to fathom his fate:
a place where stone grows wild, carrying out her fragrant rituals:
incense, the smell of devotion,
gripping the cracks, becoming eternity.
He descended the hills, removed the cloak
and pointed to his thin body as proof
of joy. The excess that bedevils our lives, all
that remains untouched, lost inside, he said when they
asked about justice. Whatever gets
here, eventually finds its place. Don't ask to win,
he told them as they stood up. Did he guess his name
would become a tool of violence?
A slow walk down the street, the stalls
upturned, the placing of death between him
and others. I think about him turning his head
to bless—I expected that light—turning
his cheek, writing a final line: whatever finds its place
loses it to the earth.

BABEL: THE IMMIGRANT SPEAKS

Nothing prepares you for being foreign. Nothing
remains of home, the last vessels are shattered,
the rules broken. Children no longer know
the names. You want to place it, but it's always misplaced.
The river and the animals hint there is someone
to complain to, someone to tell of lost fragrances.
Dissimilation, sweet-talking and lies: a new language.
Nothing prepares you for death
far away from where you are.
Suddenly you're living there,
eating fruit under wraps
by a reservoir, walking down
a long path toward a well, falling asleep in the grass.
Nothing prepares you
for the twilight;
you revisit somewhere that does not exist
and all of a sudden you're in the right place.

THE KHAZAR KINGDOM

In the depths of our hearts
we welcomed an outburst,
capitulation of the idea of one God, one nation,
an end to the hounding. Alienation prevents us going door
to door, city to city, with books and passion, handing out pamphlets
with an urgency reserved for those who claim humanity
can only be saved through a single psalm.
Pride? Racism? Those reasons glitter too brightly. It's loneliness,
that same quality Abraham presented to history, wandering
toward a distant land. But here, in the kingdom of Khazar,
they draw closer. What attracts them to the secret cult
whose strength lies in stories, an instinct for drama, an unbroken affinity
with words? The knowledge that they simply endure remains unexplained.
The body is a mysterious site, a treacherous one.
Better if it had walked away, leaving the soul
to hover above the sorrow of bones and yet,
hunched over, we traverse history.
it seems the promise was the explanation—
a white-cloaked enters a city—the end
of quarreling, sitting under an open sky,
dwelling in a land with the clime of the sublime.

MARTIN BUBER

We face each other, I and thou.
The stories, where are they? Fables
in which light penetrates the face
of a Jew crushed by climate, fatigue,
distance. That's what you intended, no?
The way everything disappears
and only the gaze remains. I agree
with you: God is a collection of voices
calling out. There's no point signing documents,
no point protecting yourself within the crowd,
mouthing Amen in unison. Did we reach each other yet?
I give myself over to you, preferring the immediate
over the continuous, going to synagogue
faithlessly, always about to leave. Loving
language, traveling at night when amnesia falls,
dancing the body, remaining seated
when everything ends, always sure
there is one more thing left to say.

ROSA LUXEMBURG

Who knows when she saw them for the first time,
their skin stained with coal, a river of weeds
moving slowly toward the promise. When did reading
translate into bruises on the body?
She charged into language as if summer existed
in winter. We watched the gold burn,
we clenched our fists. They laughed and kicked her
in the head, wolves driving themselves away
from themselves by howling. Her name is stitched
into our coats, her image stands in the empty
square, waiting for the hungry. There's no need
for fists or fire. Just stand there, opening
the horizon with your anthem. They're singing,
she whispered as the blood leaked away, lying
in a ditch among the weeds, hearing them
move like wild grass toward her.

GOLDA MEIR

The meetings, the journeys, the drafts and the signings,
the cunning that lies at the base of politics, the betrayal
at the base of cunning. One can only guess the strength
needed to ignore the whispering, the tight line of men,
the scorn wreathed in smiles. Here we are,
approaching the cursed year of '72, the generals entering
and exiting, the endless lists, the blood-drenched airport,
the ripped helicopter, and then '73 with maps
in stacks, troops moved this way
and that, your fatal error. After that, a hollow functioning
of the body, sitting in your room while summer boiled the blood
of young men, their empty brothers crowded together, rising
from the desert crater: the shape of the landscape suits the soul.

HANNAH ARENDT, JERUSALEM 1961

The chill. His face through the glass.
I forgive him, forgive them all for my own sake,
the sake of a new beginning, an emptying
of the letter box. Devoid of a place to call
home, a place to undress, to lie down in.
Late in the evening Jerusalem is covered in mythical logic.
Afraid, until we are ready to do anything.
I await the last parade past ancient stones.
The borders remain,
the passports, the dogs within and without.
The night remains too, the lamp, the pages.
They march outside my window, trampling the grass,
shouting to fill the air, not to hear
their own emptiness. The stench of burning rises from
the other side of nineteen forty-five.

MY FATHER, MEIR BERG

The time has come to talk with temperance.
You enumerate claims. This life
was not what you wanted, and now it dissipates.
It's too late to win, too late to beat the evil specters,
but now you call them by their first names.
You were forced to cross the ruins of war,
the ruins of communism, the ruins of family
until it turned into acerbity.
I won't go quietly, your eyes say.
Literature saved you, it saved me too,
Our faithful friends beside the bed,
fighting on behalf of us in the dust
that camouflages the real.
You gave them to me.
Can I ask for an interlude for you?
Years in a cramped living room, surrounded by books,
relighting your pipe, summer vacations
on plastic chairs by the Black Sea,
a long swim toward the horizon,
a full plate, good wine, fatigue,
a slow emptying.

MY MOTHER, SHOSHANA OPPENHEIMER-BERG

The time has come to talk with temperance.
You stay within the boundaries of domesticity
while I pull away, hearing voices
from over the hills. No, I found
nothing, but there are always other hills.
The good deeds protect you,
the cakes for births and weddings.
Generosity opens us,
hushing the dogs of loneliness.
I don't know how to give the simple stuff—
sugar, flour, friendship—
only a stubborn melody about a hike to the hills.
I disappoint you
and the light relaxes
leaving us here in the summer
softness of the hill.

Part V

HUNGRY
AND
SURGING

A FIRST ENCOUNTER WITH DEATH

I entered the house after evening prayers. My father
was making Havdalah. A strange silence, an unfamiliar one,
circumvented my brother, my mother, my father
too, frozen inside themselves, unmoving.
The Sabbath dissolved, everything achieved
at prayers—independence, reflection and introspection—
all of that was crushed like a note there is no need for
and something frozen passed through me too.
My grandfather had died, I don't recall who said it
but I remember leaving the room, crumpling
behind a heater, planning my revenge in detail.
I heard my mother gathering clothes, sheets,
preparing for the seven long days of her life.
They searched me out, and Grandpa Yitzhak
passed through the house, looking for me too,
twisting his hand in the motion of learning Talmud.
They shouted my name but only he whispered,
drawing near and dissipating, like a flickering sun.
I talked to him until my eyes became heavy
and he drew close one last time,
passing soft hands over my head. I fell asleep,
and from an empty room he beckoned me,
leaning over the Talmud, to come.

SAMARIA

The journey continues, the years upturn the land,
what was noon in the shade of a fig tree, deep in the valley's basin,
has become an arid hill. The vineyard
is left alone to work its sweetness, the sun wanders
over the antiquities of Ai but the eye is drawn to signs
of disaster: barbed wire, concrete watchtowers,
graffiti on the houses of Ramallah. Someone scurries about
barefoot, staining his Shabbat shirt with seraph,
coming back with the gift of burst fruit, the resin
flowing. He sees the village houses,
hears the streaming water,
a boy gathering fury, dreaming of dust
rising up from the blow.
The years upturn the land,
converting the bending asphalt into bypass roads,
the lookout towers into classrooms where pupils sit, planning
their escape, gripping the metal of their hearts.
What will be with the boy,
with twilight relaxing the day's violence, placing the sheet of darkness
on the shoulders of the land, allowing the eye to see
wild shapes in the grove, its branches a delicate dance
in the air, the rotting of fermented fruit, water pooling,

descending the terraces. What will be
when the eye both loves and hates,
when the hand registers the sweetness, the injustice
and a promise that was never made.

PARTING THE SEA

Night climbs, arrives abruptly.
Statues grow cold, lose power.
Scraps of bread collect air, drying
mouthless, too late to turn back.
Breaths appear from nowhere and then
a coat and a body, a swift move
toward the stairs, a flash of electricity,
stale blankets. The statues are shapeless,
the leaders doubled over.
What flows now, will also evanesce,
whirling light and shadow, whirling
stone and flesh. I sit, body motionless.
Night climbs up my limbs, wide awake,
warmed through, crossing the sea ruinously.

REPORT FROM A FREE CITY

In the darkness whose name is soul we call,
moving startled hands, trying to hold on.

Towns burn inside the night,
barren light on their faces.

Who lies within us, making noise of metal?
Who is so thirsty he crawls?

Ships return without gold.
In rooms, holy ones shine

on peeling walls
and in the travesty whose name is family

we advance alone.
Only the dead embrace us

as we sleep. Autumn
and Spring are squandered.

Hunger sharpens the senses,
The olive tree stoops.

We eat quickly and on the balcony
plants lean forward, long-necked, into the sun.

INTERLUDE

Oranges burn on the kitchen table.
On the radio, because of the riots, they're playing
that blue gray tune.

Dusk within dusk, the soul and the darkness.
A hand around a cup, steam curling,
days burning, the other hand peels away the skin

of the orange. A pungent smell.
Nectar shatters on the wooden table,
night has fallen without my knowledge.

The shouting through the wall has passed.
Each slice of orange posits a different facet
of orphanhood

created from iron, a desire for a fist
rising up from the east, barbed wire and concrete.
I hear the voice of the one

who came down
from the hill.
Euterpe, all in white.

RED

You let it sink in, find yourself again
in that same stage setting—a glass and a bottle of wine,
a book by Lorca, music on the radio.
Is this your father again, the creaking door,
those four paces between door and bed,
that breathing? Are these the nights following
the same attempt to annihilate touch
by touch, to keep going forward and backward
like a dark prayer, like an obstinate flickering,
a trapped firefly? Listen to the rain in the evening
as it wanders empty streets.
Howl of jackals, the electric arteries
of the city, partygoers shrieking laughter and smoke.
You are a stone on the rock-bed of night, one hand
on the stomach, the other fisted over your eyes.

DANA

I awake to you reading, your hand
sweeping hair from your eyes. I rest my cheek
on your neck, the smell of sweat,
witness to how we fell asleep.

Your hand moves across me. I fall asleep
again, awakening to olive oil
spitting in a pan, to lemon and mint leaves,
to bread in the toaster. You hum Leonard.

I gaze at you from the kitchen door, in my underwear.
The street and the cars, a single siren.
One hand mixes tahini, tastes.
The other rests on the countertop, naked.

INTERIM REPORT

I think beyond the mountains, beyond
the flesh, the green pasture
where something halts
so the eternal will emerge. Praying while
thinking about lost moments, talking while
thinking about prayer, a deadly attraction
toward death and night, fig and olive.
I do not notice my parents climbing alone
up the mountain, or the upturned garbage cans,
the ravenous vapor rising in the south like a plague.
The fire, the other one, barely scorched me,
but the tired embers still whisper,
rising up from a flickering flame.

LOVE

The evening rests a soft hand
on the shoulders of the slopes.
They tremble for a moment,
then succumb.
The dog strays for a while then
returns to rest at my feet, panting,
waiting for a sign.
Back then I slept on iron beds,
dreaming of long roads.
Other boys slept beside me, wilting
in the close air of the tent, guns at rest.
The dog senses my despair rising up,
stubborn as the thorny bushes growing
in the *wadi*, spreading everywhere.
He rouses himself and draws closer,
allowing his heavy breath to mingle
with mine, reminding me how,
in the old house, we wrestled together
on the grass, and how we grew together.
The darkness releases cold from the rocks,
flames of electricity erupt from the houses.
The dog gets up, hearing the rustle of rabbits,
but gives up, supressing the instinct
and thrusting his face into my open hands,

nudging them with his snout. In his canine heart
he knows I must return to the army
so he brings me twigs, pebbles,
and begins to play.

WALKING

The wind struck everything, the water contorted
this way and that: the sea moved inside itself
like the murmurings of a madman. Some rowed there:
the surfers' colors diluting into gray.
Through the frail light I saw a flock of birds,
sculpting dark lines of a journey home,
doubtless tired, waiting for the brassy sun
to warm their backs. I saw the hubris,
the frenzy to move faster: my own body
for whom home is something else —
empty, diaphanous, made of memory. The fishermen
folded up into layers of fabric,
the wind in their faces betraying patience,
tension. I walked swiftly to Jaffa —
not to the stone buildings, not the watchtowers,
nor the vapors of the sweet orchid —
but to the ancient within me, the other city.

EPILOGUE

The lake is revealed where the sky withdraws.
Twilight lifts, water coalesces
into an opaque gleaming rock.
November. Through naked trees,
through village houses
kitchen windows are illuminated.

Weeds surge through the night
like gossamer, like quicksilver
to my unknowing eyes.
I light a campfire,
recall an act of love, in the Himalayas,
snowflakes descending around us.

Afterward I dip in the waters,
my body swallowed up and disappearing,
autumn leaves swept down into the deep.
Like them I have nothing to grasp, located
in this season of urgency,
drawing near to the continuance, blue.

ACKNOWLEDGMENTS

Sincere thanks to the Rothschild Foundation
and Haim Goldgrabber for their support.

Sincere gratitude to the editors of the following
journals in which these translations first appeared,
sometimes in different forms: *Consequence, Ilanot
Review, Lunch Ticket, Mantis, Oomph: Contemporary
Works in Translation, Northwest Review of Books,*
and *Poetry International.*

Special thanks to Rafi Weichert, Hebrew editor
and publisher.

ABOUT THE AUTHOR

YONATAN BERG is a leading Hebrew poet. He
is the youngest recipient of the Yehuda Amichai
Prize and a number of other national awards. He
has published three books of poetry, one memoir,
and two novels. His latest book, *Far from the Linden
Trees*, was published in 2018 and received excellent
reviews. Yonatan Berg is a bibliotherapist and
teaches creative writing in Jerusalem.

ABOUT THE TRANSLATOR

JOANNA CHEN is a literary translator and
essayist whose work has been published in
numerous international journals. Her translations
include Agi Mishol's *Less Like a Dove* (2017) and
Meir Shalev's *My Wild Garden* (2019).